WHERE? IN THE wild World

DISCOVER WHERE TO FIND SOME OF THE RAREST AND MOST DANGEROUS BUGS!

ENDANGERED

MANY OF THE INSECTS FEATURED IN THIS BOOK ARE THREATENED WITH EXTINCTION. WHAT CAN YOU DO TO SAVE THEM?

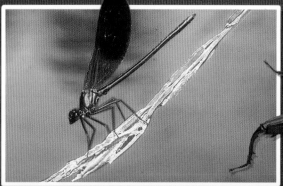

LEARN ALL ABOUT SOME OF THE WORLD'S MOST INCREDIBLE CREATURES!

THE PICTURES WITH THE HIGH DEFINITION LOGO ON THEM CAN BE SEEN IN AMAZING FULL COLOR 3D WHEN YOU PUT ON YOUR HIGH DEFINITION GLASSES.

HOW TO USE YOUR HIGH DEFINITION 3D GLASSES

The Goliath is the world's heaviest beetle – heavier than a pack of cards!

Beetles

BEETLES can live nearly everywhere – except in the oceans. They are not fussy eaters, as they will nibble on just about anything, including wood, carpets and other animals' droppings! Under their hard wing-cases, nearly all beetles have a pair of wings neatly packed away. Even water-beetles have wings that help them get from one pond to another.

In some countries, shiny Scarab beetles are worn as living jewelery.

Atlas beetle, armed and dangerous!

Some longhorn beetles are long-bodied too. This South American Longhorn is over six inches long!

IT'S A FACT:
There are over 50,000 species of beetle in the world!

Fireflies aren't flies at all, they are actually beetles. To attract each other they create light from their abdomens using a special chemical.

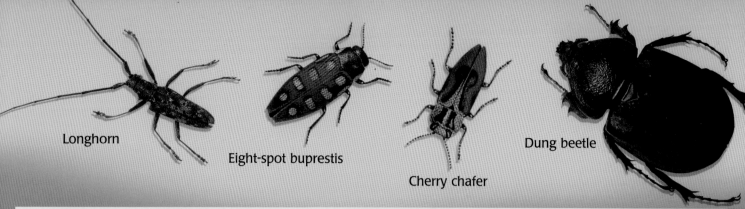

Longhorn

Eight-spot buprestis

Cherry chafer

Dung beetle

HIGH DEFINITION 3D

Like other adult insects, beetles breathe through a network of airpipes that run throughout their bodies. Even water-beetles, like the one pictured above, need air. These beetles swim to the surface and breathe out a bubble of stale air before taking in a fresh supply!

WHERE? IN THE wild World

COLORADO BEETLE
NORTH AMERICA and FRANCE

THE WORLD'S MOST WANTED BEETLE

Before people began growing potatoes in the Rocky Mountains, the Colorado beetle lived there quietly on a diet of buffalo-bur leaves But it soon developed a taste for the newly planted potatoes. It has now become a dreaded pest wherever potatoes are grown

5

MEXICAN RED-KNEE TARANTULA
With a legspan over 10 inches, this spider is
as big as a dinner plate!

Spiders

Size isn't a problem for this spider. In fact, most spiders will happily tackle prey bigger than themselves.

An ORB WEAVER is attracted by the vibrations its prey is making while it struggles to escape from the sticky web.

WITH eight legs, spiders aren't insects, although they are related to them. Many different types of spiders spin silk to make webs. Though finer than a human hair, spider's silk is extremely strong. Web spiders use this hi-tech material to build sophisticated webs of all different shapes and sizes, designed for one purpose – to catch a meal!
And they do a good job because spiders help control many pests and other insects that would otherwise devour crops and spread disease.

IT'S A FACT:

Spiders are great at recycling. When rebuilding or repairing their webs, they eat the old silk as they go along!

This wolf spider has an egg sac attached to its abdomen. When the eggs hatch, the spiderlings hitch a lift on their mother's back until they are old enough to go out on their own!

Flower spider

Zebra spider

Black widow

Red back

Striped crab spider

Swamp spider

HIGH DEFINITION 3D

A Wolf spider eyes up the 'dish of the day'!

WHERE? IN THE wild World

FUNNEL-WEB SPIDER
AUSTRALIA

FIENDISH FANGS

The Australian funnel-web is one of the world's most deadly spiders. Its bite can even be lethal to humans. If a small mammal or lizard trips one of the strands of silk connected to its underground funnel-shaped web, the waiting spider senses the vibrations and strikes with deadly speed!

Butterflies

A Queen Alexandra birdwing measures 10 inches across, making it the largest butterfly in the world.

A silver-studded blue displays its iridescent coloring.

THERE are over 15,000 species of butterfly around the world. They are similar to other insects – six legs, a head, thorax and abdomen. But what makes them special is that their wings have thousands of tiny scales. These colorful scales create different types of patterns, making them some of the most beautiful creatures on Earth.

A brilliantly colored peacock.

Swallowtail caterpillar

The owl butterfly has a very appropriate name and keeps alive by making itself look larger than it actually is!

IT'S A FACT:
A caterpillar eats enough to increase its weight 1,000 times before hatching.

With hundreds of species around the world, swallowtails are among the most common type of butterfly. Swallowtails have elongated tails that look like the tail of a certain type of bird, the swallow. They use these tails to confuse predators. When they fold their wings, these tails look like antennae, tempting the predator to attack the wrong end and increase the chances that the butterfly will survive!

HIGH DEFINITION 3D

Monarch butterfly feeding.

MONARCHS ON THE MOVE

Monarch butterflies are very accomplished travelers. When the climate turns colder in the fall, they set out from their North American homeland and fly south. Some 2,500 miles later they reach their winter homes in California and Mexico.

MONARCH BUTTERFLY
NORTH AMERICA

Moths

Death's head hawk moth – superstitions surround this spooky night flyer.

THERE are many, many more species of moths than butterflies, and their caterpillars eat a wider variety of foods. In addition to leaves, moths have developed a taste for things as diverse as wood, wax, fruit, fur and even feathers! Most moths fly at night, so spotting them can be tricky. If you use a bright light to attract them, you should be rewarded with some spectacular finds! Although it can be difficult to distinguish some moths from butterflies, there are some fundamental differences. Most butterflies are colorful and have their wings closed when settled, while moths are generally duller in color and rest with their wings outstretched.

Camouflage plays a big part in a moth's survival.

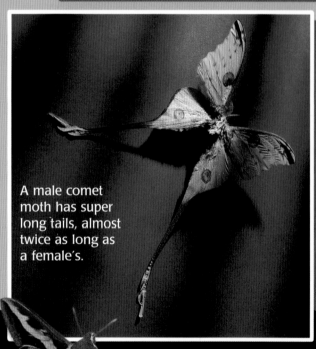

A male comet moth has super long tails, almost twice as long as a female's.

These hawk moths can reach speeds in excess of 30 miles per hour – speedy indeed!

The hummingbird hawk moth is so named because it hovers while using its extra-long tongue to sip nectar, rather than settling on its food plants like most other moths.

IT'S A FACT:

Some moths have an incredible sense of smell – a male Emperor moth can detect a female more than six miles away!

A false silk moth and a Chinese silk moth – similar, but different.

The IO moth is also known as the Bull's Eye moth.

With a wingspan of six inches, the Cecropia is the largest moth to be found in North America.

WHERE? IN THE Wild World

MEGA MOTH

ATLAS MOTH
INDIA and SOUTH-EAST ASIA

With a wingspan of up to 12 inches, Atlas moths are the giants of the moth world. They are often raised for the silk that can be made of their larvae.

Flies

THE NAME 'fly' really applies to an insect with only one pair of wings. This group includes gnats, midges, and mosquitoes. Strictly speaking, with two pairs of wings, dragonflies and damselflies are not true flies. Another difference is the way they feed. True flies can only consume liquid food, but dragons and damsels are predatory, feeding on other insects. Flies have evolved to be quite adaptable, and some feed by injecting their targets with digestive juices and then sucking up the liquified meat. Thankfully, some, like hoverflies, are much more friendly – feeding on nectar instead.

Tropical dragonfly

Some flies prey on smaller flies.

A nectar-loving beefly.

This is a damselfly. It rests with wings closed. A resting dragonfly has its wings open.

A dragonfly emerges from its nymph case like something from a sci-fi film.

A vegetarian hoverfly.

IT'S A FACT:

Flies can only eat liquid food, so they have to dissolve solids with their vomit before sucking it up!

Hoverflies

Horseflies

Hoverflies mimic wasps to make potential predators think they are more dangerous than they actually are. Meanwhile, female Horseflies are like stealth bombers – they land secretly before biting and sucking the blood of their victim.

HIGH DEFINITION 3D

Face-to-face with a robber-fly!

SMALL BUT DEADLY MENACE

WHERE?
IN THE
Wild
World

MALARIA MOSQUITO
TROPICAL AFRICA, ASIA and AMERICA

Malaria, one of the world's most dreaded human diseases, is transmitted by the bite of the female Anopheles mosquito.

Grasshoppers and Crickets

Baby crickets are tiny wingless versions of their parents.

Q. How does a cricket survive in the dark?

A. Cave-dwelling crickets make up for a serious lack of vision by using their super-sensitive antennae to find food and water.

IT'S A FACT:

Some grasshoppers can jump the human equivalent of two football fields!

Each type of cricket has a unique song so as to attract only females of the same species.

Green bush-cricket

These bugs have built-in camouflage. They blend in with leaves or bark to hide!

The tropical stick insect can grow up to an amazing 20 inches long!

A thorny Asian stick insect.

Close-up of a locust's head.

GRASSHOPPERS and crickets, together with cockroaches, stick insects and mantises, make up a very ancient group of insects. These insects are mostly vegetarian and have powerful jaws for slicing through leaves. Many species are hard to spot even though they may be large. Unlike other insects, grasshoppers and crickets are very noisy. The males make their mating song by rubbing a rough part of their thigh against a wing-case. Their ears are on their legs, too! But being noisy doesn't make them any easier to find, because it is very hard to tell which direction the sound is coming from!

HIGH DEFINITION 3D

Grasshoppers are divided into two main groups: long-horned ones like this and short-horned ones like locusts.

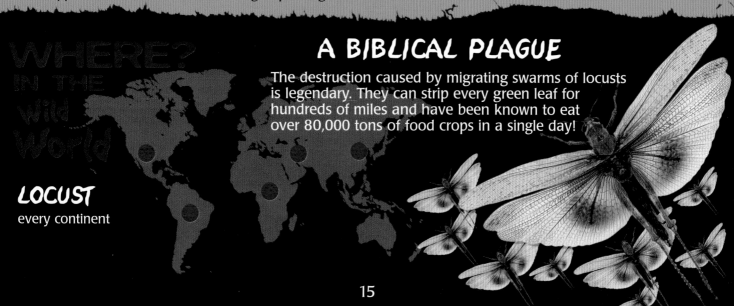

WHERE? IN THE Wild World

A BIBLICAL PLAGUE

The destruction caused by migrating swarms of locusts is legendary. They can strip every green leaf for hundreds of miles and have been known to eat over 80,000 tons of food crops in a single day!

LOCUST
every continent

Overripe fruit is a big attraction for wasps.

Wasps and Bees

BEES are possibly the most important of insects. Without them, over half of the plants we cultivate would not be pollinated and therefore would not produce seeds. Without bees, many fruit and vegetable crops would die out!

Pollen collection in progress.

A spider-hunting wasp attacks a spider.

There are some species, like this halicitid bee, that are solitary, preferring to live alone rather than in large colonies.

A difference between bees and wasps is the stinger, which is straight and smooth in a wasp but jagged in a bee. Wasps can survive after using their sting, but a bee's sting cannot be withdrawn so the bee loses a part of its body and dies.

IT'S A FACT:
A honeybee colony can contain up to 80,000 workers!

16

Some bumblebee colonies have fewer than 20 bees!

Buff-tailed bumblebee

Although hornets are the largest species of wasp, they are in fact the least aggressive and will only sting if threatened.

BEES and wasps (plus their close relatives the ants) are among the most amazing insects in the world. Although many species live alone, most live in huge, highly-organized societies. Bee and wasp societies revolve around one or more queens – fertile females that spend their entire life laying eggs. The other members of the colony care for the larvae, hunt for food, and build, repair and defend the nest. All these workers are females. The only job for males is fertilizing the new queens, just once in a lifetime.

HIGH DEFINITION 3D

Wasps use wood chewed into paper to build their nests.

WHERE? IN THE Wild World

AFRICAN 'KILLER' BEES

from AFRICA to BRAZIL and now CALIFORNIA

ADVANCE OF THE KILLER BEES?

In 1956, the Brazilian government crossed some bad-tempered but very productive African bees with some ordinary honeybees. The aggressive crossbreeds escaped and have been moving north for over fifty years. They are more likely to sting than any other species of bee, but are hardly 'killers'.

Megabugs

MANY insects have some sneaky tricks for trapping their neighbors! Mantises blend in with their surroundings until some unsuspecting little fly or beetle comes within reach of those two lightning-quick front legs. Once captured, there is no escape. Most of the 4,000 species of assassin bugs stick to stabbing other insects, but a small number – known as 'kissing bugs' – also bite people. The bad news is that, as well as being very painful, their bite can carry some deadly tropical diseases.

An assassin bug lies in wait for an unsuspecting victim!

Poison is the weapon of choice for this tarantula.

Praying or preying mantis?
With its front legs ready
to strike, it looks like this mantis is
praying for a meal!

Common centipedes have around thirty legs, but some tropical species have more than a hundred. Their front legs have claws designed to inject poison that can paralyse prey much larger than the centipede itself!

IT'S A FACT:

Mantises are meat-eating cousins of grasshoppers and stick insects.